BEFORE YOU BEGIN...

Make sure to download the FREE audio program for this book which comes with your purchase! Just go to

www.slangman.com/audio

then look for your book and enter this code:

E2H1VLULAIAN

Written by: David Burke
Copy Editor: Nili Hirsch and
Tami Kamin-Meyer
Illustrated by: "Migs!" Sandoval
Translator: Ofra Obejas
Proofreader: Kai Cofer

Copyright © 2017 by David Burke

Email: info@heywordy.com
Website: www.heywordy.com

Hey Wordy! and all related characters and elements are © and trademarks of Hey Wordy, LLC.

Published by Slangman Publishing. Slangman is a registered trademark of David Burke. All rights reserved. Reproduction or translation of any part of this work beyond that permitted by section 107 or 108 of the 1976 United States Copyright Act without the permission of the copyright owner is unlawful. Requests for permission or further information should be addressed to the Permissions Department, Slangman Publishing. This publication is designed to provide accurate and authoritative information in regard to the subject matter covered. The persons, entities and events in this book are fictitious. Any similarities with actual persons or entities, past and present, are purely coincidental.

ISBN13: 978-1-891888-40-3

Printed in the U.S.A.

Meet the Author
David Burke

Creator and star of the children's TV show, *Hey Wordy!*, David Burke has been single-handedly revolutionizing the foreign language-learning movement worldwide.

In addition to being a performer of boundless energy and enthusiasm, David speaks seven languages. A successful author and entrepreneur, he has built a thriving international publishing company featuring over 100 books he has written for teen/adults & children. His books have won publishing awards and have sold more than one million copies. David's Street Speak™ and Biz Speak™ series of books and audio programs are used around the world by government agencies, leading universities and major corporations.

Since age 4, David has been a classically trained pianist and uses his musical gifts to compose and perform original songs for his TV series, *Hey Wordy!* which introduces children to foreign languages and cultures through music, animation, and magical adventures. He has also composed, orchestrated, and performed all the music in the audio programs for each of these books.

David's engaging and charismatic persona became a fixture on broadcast entertainment channels around the world, such as CNN and the BBC. David and his work have been highlighted in many major publications, including The Los Angeles Times, The Chicago Tribune and The Christian Science Monitor.

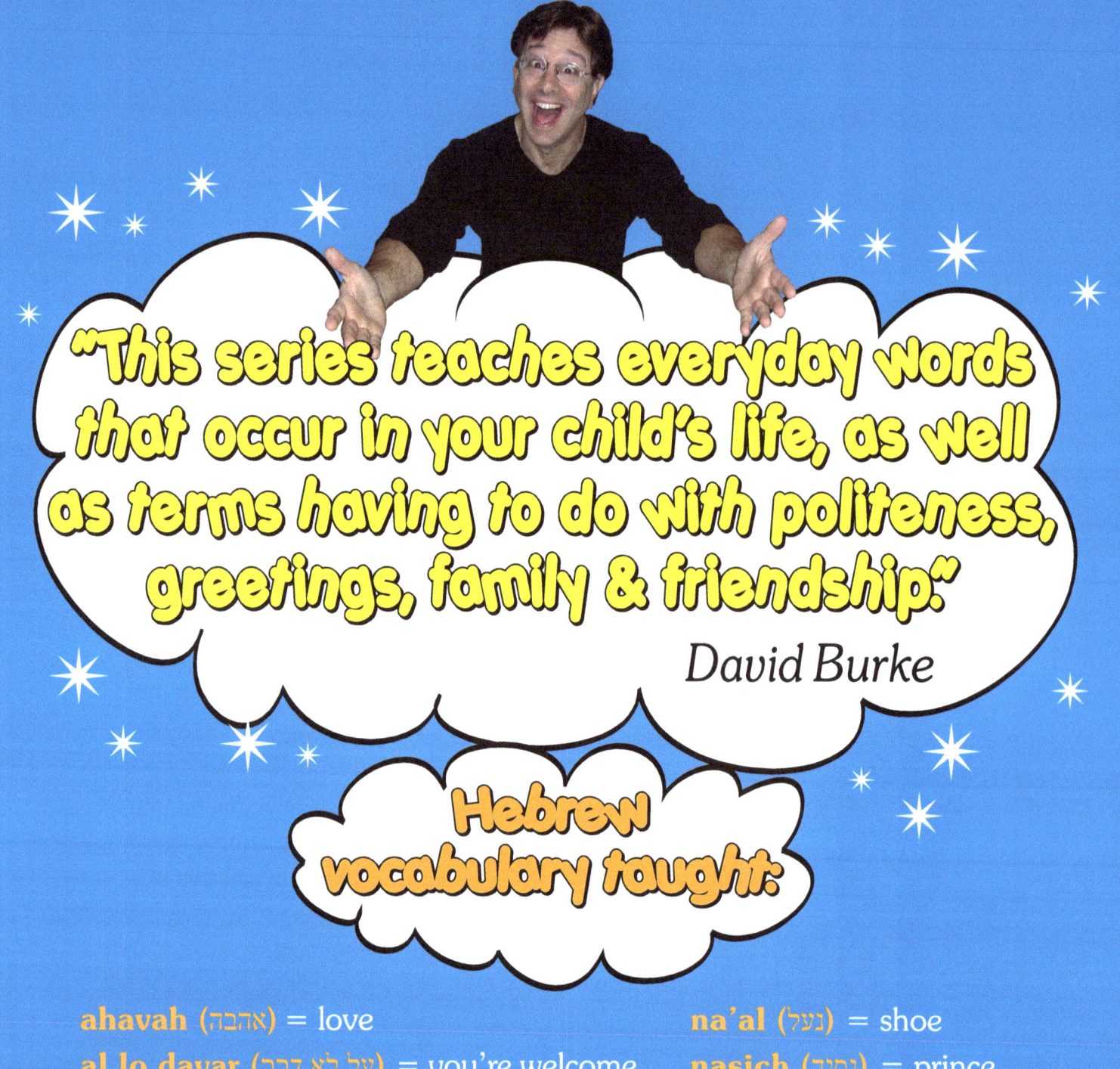

"This series teaches everyday words that occur in your child's life, as well as terms having to do with politeness, greetings, family & friendship."

David Burke

Hebrew vocabulary taught:

ahavah (אהבה) = love
al lo davar (על לא דבר) = you're welcome
atzuvah (עצובה) = sad
bayit (בית) = house
chatzot (חצות) = midnight
gdola (גדולה) = big
ishah (אישה) = wife
kaf regel (כף רגל) = foot
le'hitra'ot (להיתראות) = goodbye
mesibah (מסיבה) = party
na'al (נעל) = shoe
nasich (נסיך) = prince
ra'ah (רעה) = mean
rega (רגע) = moment
simlah (שמלה) = dress
smechah (שמחה) = happy
todah (תודה) = thank you
yafah (יפה) = pretty
yafeh (יפה) = handsome
yaldah (ילדה) = girl

Dedication

The entire "Foreign Language Through Fairy Tales" series is dedicated to all the children of the world.

It is through their understanding, appreciation, and celebration of our differences that the world will become a better and safer place for us all.

yaldah ילדה

yafah יפה

bayit בית

Once upon a time, there lived a teenage [girl] named Cinderella who was very [pretty]. The **yaldah**, who was very **yafah** lived in a small [house] with her

stepmother and two stepsisters. At times it was difficult for the **yaldah** to live in such a small **bayit** with her stepmother and stepsisters. Why? Because they were

ra'ah
רעה

jealous that she was so **yafah** which is why her stepmother was extra mean to her. But the poor **yaldah** never complained about living in a small

bayit with her stepmother, who was very **ra'ah**, and stepsisters, even though they forced her to do all the work in the entire **bayit** day in and day out!

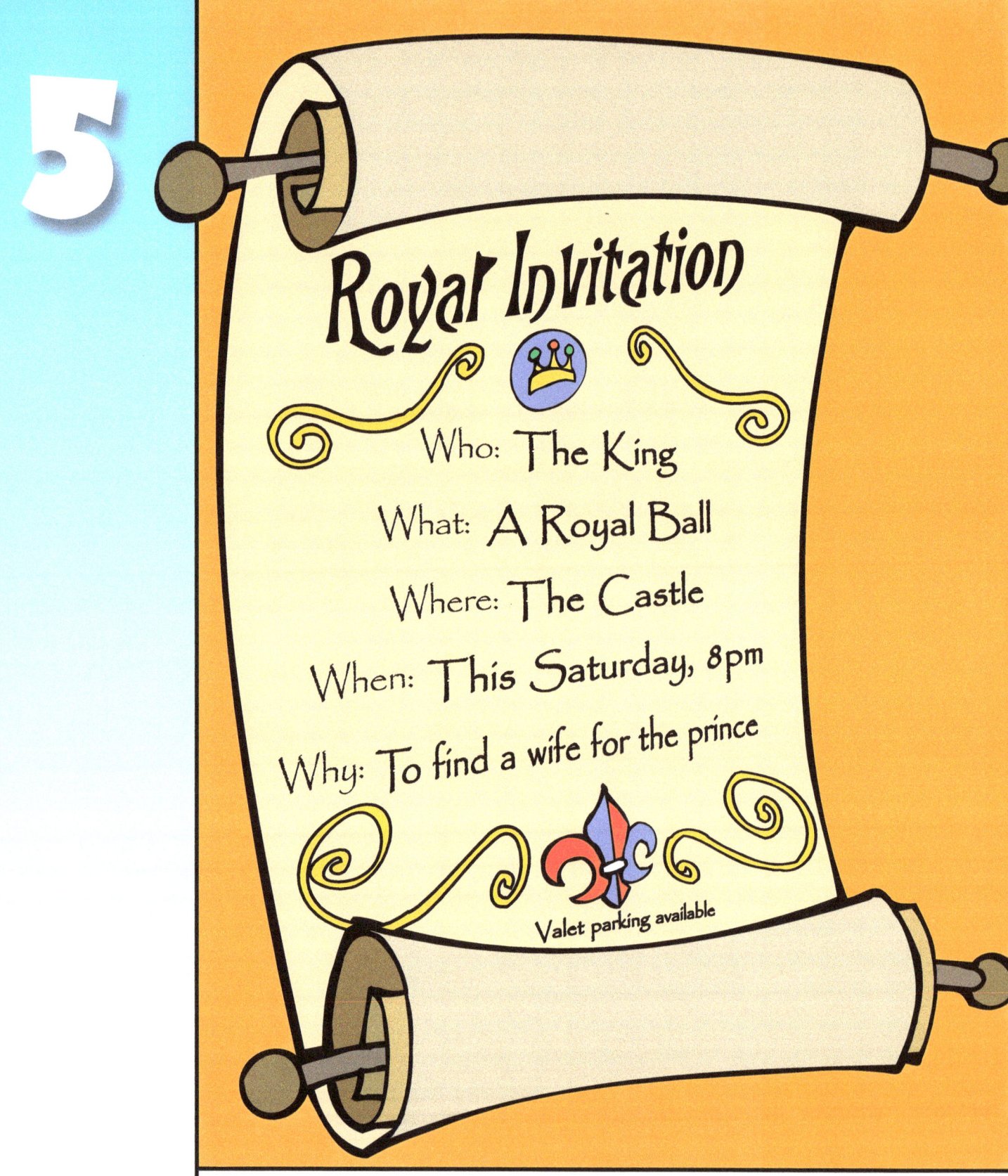

mesibah
מסיבה
gdola
גדולה

One day, a royal invitation arrived at the **bayit** of the poor **yaldah**. The king was throwing a party for the royal prince. And the **mesibah** was going to be big. The **mesibah**

was going to be *very* **gdola**! The prince was [handsome], not only **yafeh**, but kind. And every **yaldah** in the land was invited to the **mesibah** so that he could choose a [wife].

yafeh
יפה

ishah
אישה

7

nasich נסיך

The king and queen also hoped the **prince** would find an **ishah** who was truly **yafah** both inside and out. The **nasich** was very excited about his royal **mesibah**!

The night of the **mesibah** for the **nasich** arrived but Cinderella was very sad. Her stepmother was so **ra'ah**, she wouldn't let her leave the **bayit** to go to the **mesibah**!

atzuvah
עצובה

She was so **atzuvah**, she started to cry. She was the only **yaldah** not allowed to leave her **bayit** and get the chance to meet the **nasich** at the **mesibah** and become his **ishah**.

Suddenly a voice from behind her said, "My dear, I'm your fairy godmother and you'll be able to go to the **mesibah** of the **nasich** and... you'll be wearing an elegant dress!"

simlah
שמלה

And with a wave of her wand, Cinderella was now wearing the most elegant **simlah** imaginable. "Thank you! **Todah**!" exclaimed Cinderella. She was now a

Todah
תודה

yaldah who was truly **yafah**, wearing an elegant **simlah**, and eager to leave her **bayit** to meet the royal **nasich** at the **mesibah**, hoping to become his **ishah**!

13

rega
רגע

chatzot
חצות

"One moment!" the fairy godmother added. "Make sure to leave the **mesibah** by midnight because your **simlah** will change back to the way it was!"

Cinderella thought for a **rega** then said, "I will. I'll remember to leave before **chatzot**, fairy godmother." So, the **yaldah**, who was very **yafah**, left for the **mesibah**. She

smechah
שמחה

was no longer **atzuvah**, but very happy to be meeting the **nasich**. As she got out of her carriage, she could hear the **mesibah** and indeed it was **gdola**! Cinderella walked in

and wasn't too **smechah** to see more than one **yaldah** waiting to meet the royal **nasich**. But after a **rega**, she calmed down and was ready to

meet the **nasich** face to face. And indeed he was very **yafeh**! She couldn't believe her eyes! And clearly, the **nasich** felt great [love] for the **yaldah** the **rega** he saw her!

ahavah
אהבה

"**Todah** very much for inviting me to your **mesibah**," said Cinderella. "You're welcome," responded the **nasich**. Cinderella and the **nasich**

Al lo davar
על לא דבר

danced and danced for hours, until the stroke of **chatzot** was upon them which the **yaldah** had completely forgotten about! And poof! Her **simlah** vanished!

"Goodbye!" shouted Cinderella.
"**Le'hitra'ot**! And **todah** for inviting me!"
"**Al lo davar**," responded the **nasich**.
And Cinderella ran back to her **bayit**.

Le'hitra'ot
להיתראות

na'al
נעל

The only thing she left behind was a glass shoe. Since the royal **nasich** had such **ahavah** for Cinderella, he went from town to town looking for a **yaldah** whose

kaf regel
כף רגל

foot would fit the glass **na'al**. After days of eliminating **yaldah** after **yaldah**, the poor **nasich** was getting discouraged. He thought he would never find her, but he

had one more **bayit** left to visit. The **ra'ah** stepmother and two stepsisters ran out to try on the glass **na'al** but none of them had a **kaf regel** that could possibly fit.

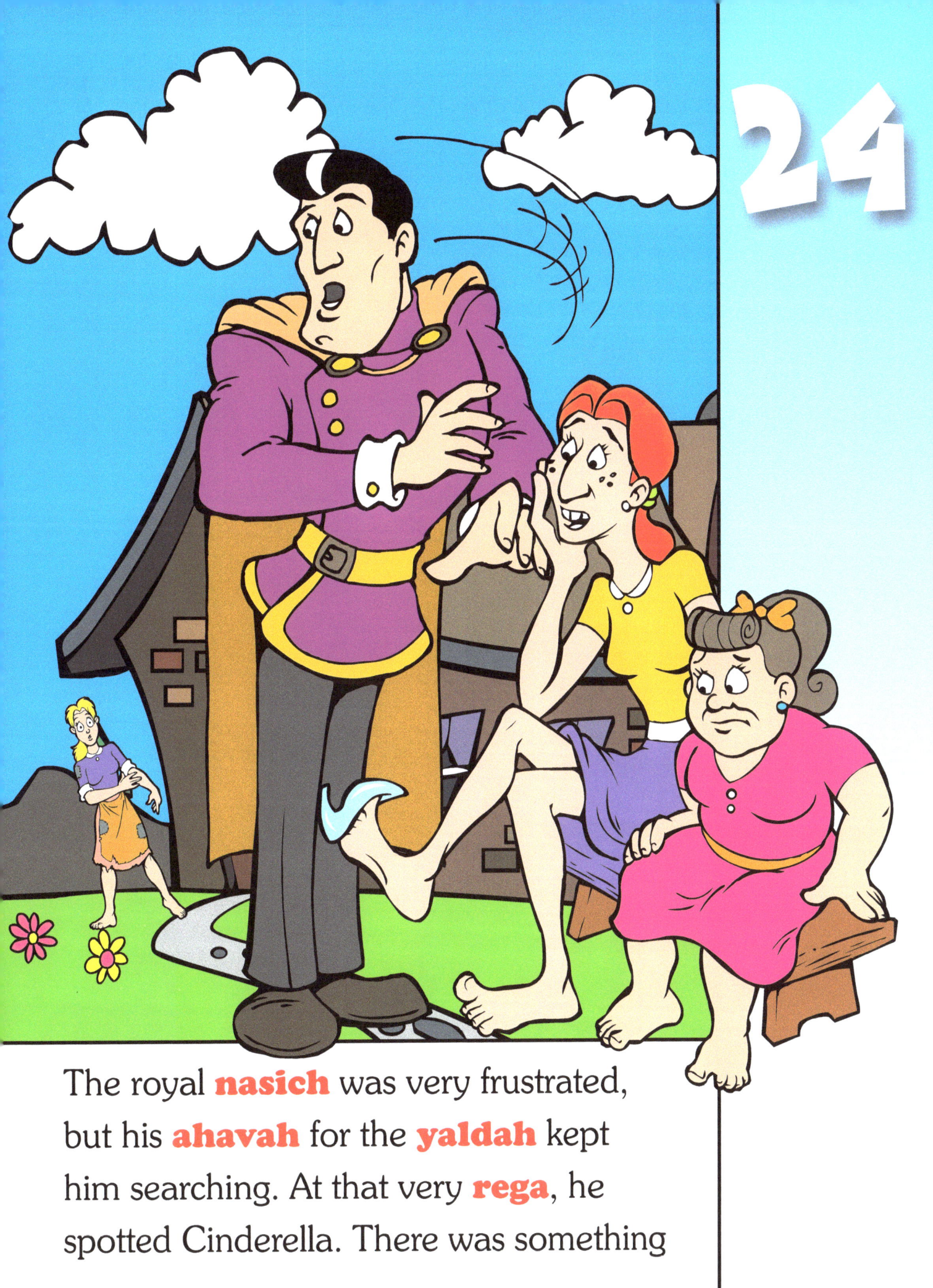

The royal **nasich** was very frustrated, but his **ahavah** for the **yaldah** kept him searching. At that very **rega**, he spotted Cinderella. There was something

very special about her. He just had to see if her **kaf regel** was the one that could fit the glass **na'al**. He knelt down in front of her and slid the **na'al** on her **kaf regel**.

And her **kaf regel** fit the glass **na'al** perfectly! At that very **rega**, Cinderella's fairy godmother reappeared and changed her back into the same **yaldah**

in the **simlah** the royal **nasich** had met at his **mesibah**. The **nasich** felt more **ahavah** for the **yaldah** than ever! And Cinderella was especially **smechah** that she lost her glass

na'al at the **mesibah** or the **nasich** may never have found her – a **yaldah** as **yafah** on the inside as on the out! Soon, Cinderella became the **ishah** of the royal **nasich**.

She was so very **smechah**! She would never, ever be **atzuvah** again. And the royal **nasich** and his **ishah**, Cinderella, lived in the castle happily ever after.

Now you're ready for Level 2!

Level 2 contains words from Level 1, plus all NEW words!

For more HEY WORDY! products, visit...

www.ingramcontent.com/pod-product-compliance
Lightning Source LLC
Chambersburg PA
CBHW042031100526
44587CB00029B/4371